P9-CET-695

Kristen Stewart
BELLA OF THE BALL!

By Jo Hurley

SCHOLASTIC INC.

New York   Toronto   London   Auckland   Sydney
Mexico City   New Delhi   Hong Kong   Buenos Aires

Photo credits:

Front cover: Patrick Rideaux/Rex USA
Back cover: Vince Bucci/Getty Images

Poster front: Michael Germana/Everett Collection
Poster back: clockwise from top left:
M.Morton/Columbia Pictures/ZUMA Press,
Chuck Zlotnick/Art Linson Productions/ZUMA Press,
Eric Charbonneau/Wireimage/Getty Images,
Christine Chew/UPI Photo/Newscom, Merrick
Morton/Columbia Pictures/ZUMAPress,
20th Century Fox/ZUMAPress

ISBN-13: 978-0-545-14110-9
ISBN-10: 0-545-14110-9

12 11 10 9 8 7 6 5 4 3 2 1   8 9 10 11 12/0

Cover and interior designed by Deena Fleming
Printed in the U.S.A.
First printing, December 2008

Introduction

How do you catch a rising star? Wait! Is that a trick question?

You can't catch a star like Kristen Jaymes Stewart. All you can do is step back and watch her blaze across the sky — and hope (fingers crossed) that you are lucky enough to have a few sparks fall down on you.

Anyone who knows Kristen would agree that since she started acting at the ripe old age of *eight*, her life has burned bright and steady. In many ways, Kristen's story reads a little bit like a Hollywood script.

Born into a showbiz family, everyone who knew her (and the Stewarts) expected she would work in showbiz, too. Her dad is a director. Her mom is a writer. Her four brothers have all been grips. (A grip is someone who helps on a movie set. See page 9 for details.) Kristen figured that showbiz was genetic. It was her destiny.

What she *didn't* expect was to get discovered, like a bolt from the blue, without any connection to her family at all.

It was kind of like a scene in a movie, actually, where a Hollywood big shot spots a pretty girl sitting at the counter in an old-fashioned drugstore and comes over with a wide smile and a cheerful, "Hello, I'd like to make you a star!"

Well, it didn't happen *exactly* like that for Kristen, but it was close. One night at school, she climbed on the stage for a performance and an agent picked her out of the crowd — just like that!

Before she could blink her long eyelashes twice, Kristen was standing in front of the camera, going for some major movie roles, and making her mark in Hollywood.

Kristen has already risen above so many strange situations:

- **The costarring role in *Panic Room* that made her a Hollywood name was originally given to another actress — but Kristen got it anyway!**

- Kristen has acted in movies that did not even make it into theaters — but she still earned rave reviews and award nominations for them!
- Kristen has acted in movies with terrible reviews — but she doesn't consider these failures!
- Kristen has faced some seriously strange stuff onscreen, including pulling off a major bank heist, living in a haunted house, being cryogenically frozen, getting a debilitating disease, and much more — and she's survived it all!
- She has costarred with almost every under-twenty-five hottie in Hollywood right now — but has never appeared on the cover of a junky supermarket tabloid!

So how does Kristen keep her star shining so bright?

For starters, she works her butt off. And when things get tough (which they often do!) she works even *harder*. That earns her tons of respect.

Another star quality: Kristen doesn't fall for paparazzi limelight. She considers her acting career a job. And she asks, "What part of a job description includes getting a photograph taken when you walk out of the supermarket?" None! Kristen digs her anonymity.

Not that she'll be able to stay anonymous for much longer! Her career is about to pop into the absolute turbosphere in late 2008 with a true career-making turn as Bella in *Twilight*. In case you haven't heard, that's the hotly anticipated movie based on the phenomenal multi-million-copy best-selling book series by author Stephenie Meyer. After *Twilight* breaks a few box office records, we'll probably be seeing Kristen on TV talk shows and in the pages of magazines like *People* — and everywhere else, too.

But no matter how much attention comes her way, we can count on one thing for sure: Kristen always plays it cool. She rarely giggles or gushes about boys or superficial stuff, at least not when the cameras are rolling. She does most of her interviews with a pleasant smile that says, *Look, I like what I do. I'm lucky and I know it*. She doesn't get overly primped or pressed for red carpet events. In her spare time, she *surfs*.

Whatever the scene, Kristen Jaymes Stewart works on keeping "real" and down-to-earth as much as possible. She's no egomaniac, not by a longshot. She's Hollywood *smart*. Kristen knows how to stay "chill" (one of her favorite expressions to describe herself and other peeps). She may as well be nicknamed Krist-*zen*!

Kristen's costar in *Twilight*, Robert Pattinson, sums it up best. He said the main reason he wanted to do the movie *Twilight* was because he wanted to work with Kristen, plain and simple. "[She's] the best actress of our generation," Robert told *MTV News*. He should know. They share some intense screen time together in the film.

Acting and directing superstar Sean Penn feels the same way about Kristen's awesome abilities. After working with her on *Into the Wild*, Sean told *Interview* magazine: "If there were a way to invest money in a career, I'd roll the dice there [with Kristen] in a big way."

Chapter 1
Born Into the Biz

W hen Kristen Stewart stepped on stage in her school's holiday revue in the late 1990s, she had no idea that her life was about to change its course — forever.

The gold, glimmering star atop the holiday scenery at school that night may have been the North Star, but another star was rising in the school auditorium that night: Kristen Jaymes Stewart.

Born April 9, 1990, in Los Angeles, California, Kristen spent most of her childhood surrounded by people in show business.

Kristen's father, John Stewart, works for FOX television. His projects include the show *On Air with Ryan Seacrest,* among others.

Her mother, Jules Mann Stewart (born in Australia),

is a scriptwriter who has worked on cable and network television shows, too. She has supervised scripts for projects like *Snow Dogs* and a new Scooby-Doo project for TV, now filming.

Even Kristen's grandfather worked in the biz a long time ago. He was reportedly an A.D. (Assistant Director) for legendary film director Cecil B. DeMille. In case you didn't know, Cecil B. DeMille is popularly known as the "King of the Epics."

Talk about an amazing family!

Standing about five feet, six inches tall, with dark brown hair and green eyes, Kristen says she always knew she would probably do *something* connected to show business. She told the Australian website girlfriend.com, "My brothers are all grips, and I grew up on craft services. [So] I always knew I would be involved somehow in film."

But how, what, and when?

She had to fill in the blanks.

Was Kristen destined to be a grip like her four brothers?

Was she going to find a life behind the camera, directing or producing the action like Dad?

Or maybe (just maybe) was Kristen destined to be

a writer? Mom supervised scripts and wrote her own original scripts. Chances were good that Kristen would inherit her mother's talent for writing — as well as her mother's work ethic.

BSS — Behind-the-Scenes Secret

You've probably seen the long list of names and jobs associated with a movie. But do you really know what all those people *do*? There are many important — and unrecognized — jobs behind the scenes of a movie set. Kristen's family members know how to do jobs like these.

Best Boy: Assists the Key Grip. If the assistant isn't actually a boy, is it Best Girl? No. It's still credited as Best Boy.

Boom Operator: Assists sound mixer by holding a long pole with a microphone out of view while cameras are rolling.

Gaffer: Person in charge of electrical stuff; also called the lighting technician.

Greensman: Decides where to put plants on a movie set.

Key Grip: Oversees the entire set, including scenery, operations, and props.

Set Dresser: Gets the set ready each day before shooting begins. A dresser has his or her own staff called the swing gang.

There was so much possibility in show business and even at a very young age, Kristen knew she had some big opportunities ahead of her. She also knew something else: No matter what part of show business she decided to pursue, it would be hard work.

The night of the holiday show at Kristen's school, the halls were decked with the expected decor — from boughs of holly to snowmen. Kids sang carols and clapped along to ringing bells. There was a rendition of the "Dreidel Song"! Kristen sang along. All in all, it was an ordinary holiday show not unlike ones at schools across the country.

Except for one thing.

Sitting there in the school auditorium audience was a powerful Hollywood agent from the Gersh Agency. And he spotted something in Kristen that he liked . . . a *lot*. As Kristen later told *Teen Vogue* magazine, "I had this obligatory little part in a school play and there was an agent in the audience. Only in L.A., right?"

Only in L.A? *Right!* Call it gut feeling or a lucky hunch, the agent sensed Kristen's superstar potential. He went after Kristen Jaymes Stewart with a plan to get her as a client. First step? The agent called Kristen's parents to ask if they were seeking "representation" for their daughter.

The agent's call took the Stewarts by surprise. After all, everyone in the family thought that Kristen might pursue a career in the entertainment industry, since she had been born into the biz. But acting? Not a chance! The Stewarts worked *behind* the camera, not in front of it.

Kristen's mother and father expressed their serious reservations to the agent — and to their daughter. But he wouldn't take no for an answer. And Kristen had to admit something she hadn't really considered before: She really *liked* performing.

"Since my parents were both in the business, [at first] they were like, 'We don't want to be stage moms,'" Kristen told Movies Online. But over time, Kristen and her parents began to reconsider the agent's offer. "[At first] we were reluctant. But then I said I would go on a couple of auditions. It just sort of snowballed."

In an interview with *Interview* magazine, Kristen admitted, "I never wanted to be the center of attention. I wasn't that 'I-want-to-be-famous, I-want-to-be-an-actor kid.' I never sought out acting, but I always practiced my autograph, because I loved pens. I'd write my name on everything."

At the tender age of eight, the Stewart family retained the Gersh Agency for their daughter. Located in the posh Beverly Hills 90210 zip code, the Gersh Agency has a reputation for young, hot clients, so expectations

All in the Family

The Stewarts are not the only ones with show business in the family blood. Several of today's top young actors are related to other folks in the biz. Below are just a few examples.

Abigail Breslin (*Kit Kittredge: An American Girl*) and brother Spencer Breslin (*The Shaggy Dog*)

Dakota Fanning (*War of the Worlds*) and sister Elle Fanning (*Daddy Day Care*)

Jake Gyllenhaal (*Donnie Darko*), sister Maggie Gyllenhaal (*The Dark Knight*), father/director Stephen Gyllenhaal, and mother/screenwriter Naomi Foner

Blake Lively (*Gossip Girl, Sisterhood of the Traveling Pants*), sister Robyn Lively (*Teen Witch*), and brother Eric Lively (*Speak* — with Kristen Stewart!)

Haley Joel Osment (*Sixth Sense*) and sister Emily Osment (*Hannah Montana*)

Emma Roberts (*Nancy Drew*), father/actor Eric Roberts, and aunt/actress Julia Roberts were high. Once she signed on, Kristen entered a wild world of auditions. She went on crazy casting calls and dove directly into the deep end of the business. The only question now was how long would it take her to make a major splash?

Right from the start, Kristen knew she had made the right decision. While many children her age were looking for a chance to play video games or hang out after school, Kristen dreamed about making movies and starring on television. She'd been discovered once at the holiday show; now all she needed was a casting director to discover her a second time — and catapult her into the public eye. How hard could that be?

Kristen's parents let go of their reservations and supported their daughter's efforts one hundred percent. If Kristen wanted to be an actress; they would do whatever they could to help her get started in the acting world. They knew the business. They *were* the business.

But nearly a year into auditions, Kristen had still not booked a role in anything — not on television, in commercials, or the movies. Kristen began to get discouraged. It was hard not to! After all, she'd been so lucky getting her agent's attention from the beginning. What more could she do to get a role?

Jon Favreau (director of *Elf*), who would later direct Kristen in the major motion picture *Zathura*, says the first thing he noticed about Kristen was her focused ability to approach acting like a job — even from a very early age. In an interview he conducted for *Interview* magazine in 2005, he told a young Kristen, "Your dad exposed you to the industry and you take it seriously. You do seem to have a lot of maturity in your decision-making . . . You really bring your lunch pail to work, so to speak. You've got a really strong blue-collar ethic about acting."

As it turns out, Kristen's work ethic mattered a lot during that first year — maybe even more than her talent. No matter what happened, Kristen would put her best foot forward and keep auditioning even when roles did not appear.

Her persistence paid off. After scores of read-throughs and cut scenes, Kristen finally got a film role. It was only a walk-on role with no lines, but that didn't make a difference. It was a step forward for Kristen. She could act! She could do this! With renewed confidence in her ability, Kristen kept auditioning and pursuing her ambition.

Kristen's very first movie was a nonspeaking part in the Disney Channel TV production *The Thirteenth Year*. She played a girl in the lunchroom. However, that role led to a small yet vital part in a new major motion picture called *The Safety of Objects*. Just like that, Kristen's career began to gain momentum.

The Safety of Objects is based on a book by award-winning author A. M. Homes. Independent director and screenwriter Rose Troche adapted Homes's many short stories into one longer movie.

In the process of making the movie, Troche changed one of the book's characters from a boy named Erol into a girl named Sam (short for Samantha). It was a lucky switch for Kristen. She eventually got the part of Sam!

The movie focuses on the intersecting lives of four families in the same suburban neighborhood. Kristen plays Sam Jennings, the tomboy daughter of the character Annette Jennings, who is played by Oscar-nominated actor Patricia Clarkson. During the course of the film, a grieving neighbor named Randy (played by popular actor Timothy Olyphant) kidnaps Sam! That kidnapping sets the stage for some major events in the film. Although Kristen has only a handful of scenes, *The Safety of Objects* gave her the opportunity to sharpen her acting skills with some of Hollywood's best and brightest.

The movie's acting ensemble stars not only Clarkson and Olyphant but also includes Academy Award–winning actress Glenn Close, Mary Kay Place, Joshua Jackson, and Dermot Mulroney. Working with this acting "family" proved as invaluable to Kristen's career as the influence of her own parents and siblings.

What mattered most about *The Safety of Objects*, however, was how it got Kristen Stewart noticed in Hollywood. After playing Sam, Kristen was considered for bigger parts — and asked to audition for a greater variety of roles. This was a very big break after a long year of not getting much work. It seemed like Kristen was on the right path at last.

Little did she know that her *biggest* break was just around the corner. . . .

Chapter 2
Panic Attack? Totally!

In 2001, Kristen and her agent heard about a role that seemed right for her. Director David Fincher was casting his new thriller *Panic Room*. He was auditioning for the part of Sarah Altman, a brooding young diabetic girl who (along with her mother) runs into serious trouble inside the walls of a New York City townhouse. Ten-year-old Kristen's short, cropped hair, smart attitude, and quiet strength were just right for the part. It was a role Kristen wanted more than anything at that time.

Fincher is a director known for a unique but simple style that includes dark themes and an atmospheric mood. His dark and moody stories are inspired by techniques from the master of drama Alfred Hitchcock. Hitchcock directed classic horror films like *Psycho*, *Rear Window*, and *The Birds*. Fincher makes serious movies with dark humor. His most famous flick is probably the hit movie *Fight Club* starring Brad Pitt.

Kristen told *Access Hollywood* that her audition for *Panic Room* was tough — and long. "I had to go back six times," she explained. "[And even then] I didn't get it!"

Instead, the part of Sarah went to up-and-coming actress Hayden Panettiere (now famous for her role as the cheerleader on the popular television show *Heroes*). But Hayden had other projects lined up. She could not fit the filming of *Panic Room* into her work schedule. She had to say no to the movie.

But what was disappointment for Hayden turned into Kristen's big break.

After Hayden backed out, Fincher went back to Kristen. As she explained to *Access Hollywood*, "[It was] two months later [after the first auditions] when they called me back."

And what happened then?

She got the part, natch. It was about time!

Kristen was in good company as a member of the *Panic Room* ensemble. The cast of the movie included famous actors like Nicole Kidman, Jared Leto, and Forest Whitaker. Nicole was cast as Meg Altman,

Just what is a *panic room* anyway?

A real-life panic room is a secure room constructed with bulletproof, explosion-proof materials; equipped with surveillance monitors, a separate phone line, and other survival aids; where residents can hide in case of emergency.

Kristen's mother, in the film. Unfortunately, Nicole, having injured herself during the filming of the hit movie musical *Moulin Rouge!*, was physically unable to do some of the stunts required by her in *Panic Room*.

A few weeks into filming, Nicole dropped out.

Without Nicole, director David Fincher was so stuck — until he learned that one of his favorite actresses, Jodie Foster, was available. (Filming on her other project *Flora Plum* had suddenly stalled.) He immediately sent Jodie the *Panic Room* script. She loved it and agreed to join Fincher's cast on short notice.

Kristen told *Interview* magazine, "Everyone always says, 'Kristen got *Panic Room* because she looks like Jodie Foster.' But it was actually Nicole Kidman who was supposed to play my mother."

Lucky for audiences, it turned out the way it did.

Jodie and Kristen seemed an ideal match. *Rolling Stone*'s movie critic Peter Travers said, "Foster and Stewart . . . forge a bond that never feels cornball." They share physical similarities from hairstyling to facial structure. They each have thoughtful eyes and lots of girl power.

Director Fincher told Cinecon.com, "When we cast Kristen Stewart, she reminded me of a young Jodie Foster. She has that sort of great droll sense of humor." So it made sense that the two would end up in the same movie! They looked like they could be a *real* mother and daughter.

Panic Room finally had a cast that not only felt right, but looked right.

When asked about her striking resemblance to Foster, Kristen told *Access Hollywood*: "My whole life people have been like, 'Oh Kristen, you look so much like Jodie Foster.' I've always been such a fan of Jodie and always looked up to her, so when I found out she was doing the movie I was really excited."

Getting Jodie on board for the film was a casting accomplishment, but it was also an incredible gift to Kristen.

Like Kristen, Jodie had been acting since she was a

young child. She won acclaim playing troubled teen-agers in movies ranging from comedies like *Freaky Friday* to intense dramas like *Taxi Driver*, which earned her an Oscar nomination at age fourteen. In recent years, she has received two best actress Academy Awards for *The Accused* and *The Silence of the Lambs*. Plus, she graduated from Yale University with a degree in literature!

When asked to name her role model, Kristen had a very simple, two-word response: Jodie Foster. At least that's what she told *Vanity Fair* magazine in 2008. In fact, naming Jodie as her idol is something Kristen has told almost *every* interviewer during her short career this far.

"Jodie Foster . . . is not just an actress," Kristen once told *Time for Kids* magazine. "She's a director, she's a producer, she's a writer. She's conquered the business. You don't see her much in the press. She's very, very well respected, very professional. She's awesome."

Jodie is a big fan of Kristen's, too.

"She really reminds me of me when I was a kid — her mannerisms, her vibe," Jodie told *Interview* magazine in 2002. "[Kristen's] approach is very different from most actors. She's stoic. She keeps it all wrapped up. Just the way she shows up on set and says hi and sticks her hands in her pockets. She's the cool girl on the block."

Naturally, the two bonded on set. In the movie, the pair spend a lot of time inside the actual "panic room" itself, an unusual space, to say the least. They were stuck together in a room with no windows for hours — and even *days*! The actresses really didn't have much of a choice about whether to be close or not. During this time, as they performed scenes in the close quarters, Fincher witnessed Jodie taking Kristen under her wing. "Having been there herself as a kid, [Jodie] knew how to disarm the anxiety of a child actor," Fincher told *USA Today*. "Jodie is so capable and fiercely intelligent. She was very nurturing."

With Jodie's help, Kristen prepared for her first big role — and for four months of serious shooting. In no time, her bad case of nerves calmed down . . . there was too much to learn to waste time being nervous!

"David Fincher does a lot of takes," Kristen told *Vanity Fair* magazine. "There was one scene we must have done eighty times. I didn't know that wasn't the norm." Performing many takes was not the only

At the start of filming *Panic Room*, Jodie Foster learned she was expecting a baby! That made the filming process tough. Jodie joked, "I did a lot of sleeping . . . I remember Kristen would make fun of me constantly because every time she would ask me what I had for lunch, [my answer] would be: Well, actually I slept through lunch."

challenge for Kristen. She had to do most of her acting inside one room. Good thing she isn't too claustrophobic!

The action scenes in the movie were a welcome relief from all of the work inside the actual panic room. Kristen told *Access Hollywood* that her favorite scene was one of Jodie's scenes — when Jodie breaks out. "There's a really suspenseful part when everybody's like, 'Oh my!' [It's] when we open the door and Jodie has to run out to get her cell phone. I love that part."

What could have been her biggest obstacle playing Sarah turned into Kristen's greatest strength in the role. She skillfully shows her character getting sicker throughout the course of the film. (Sarah is a diabetic girl separated from her insulin.) Critics marveled at how well Kristen handled the complexity of such a role. She brought skill, smarts, and sharp attention to the important details of her character.

For an actor appearing in only her *third* role, in her *first* significant part, *and* working with her screen idol (Jodie Foster), Kristen delivered a performance beyond everyone's expectations. Kristen Stewart might have only been ten years old, but she seemed wise beyond her years.

It was no big surprise then after her strong performance in *Panic Room,* that Kristen got a nomination for a Young Artist Award in the category of "Best Performance in a Feature Film — Leading Young Actress." Although she did not win the award, her confidence soared.

Kristen had so many reasons to be proud. Bit by bit, role by role, she was earning positive attention for her talent and willingness to work well with everyone.

The best was yet to come.

Chapter 3
Taking the Lead: New Movies, New Goals

"It's so great to have [*Panic Room*] do so well, really an honor," Kristen admitted to *Access Hollywood* after the flick set a box-office record on its opening weekend.

The only followup question she had was, "What *now*?"

The success of *Panic Room* got Kristen noticed by a variety of important filmmakers. It opened up new opportunities for her next movie roles. Because Kristen was concerned about being stereotyped into typical "tween" movie roles, she looked for projects that stretched her acting chops.

Kristen told *Teen Ink*, "The movies I've been interested in have been because of the prospect of working with the filmmaker and a certain director . . . I think it's important to do movies that are worth watching, something that makes you think."

"It's nice when you can see a young teenage girl actually get up and kick butt and empower herself," Kristen explained to movieline.com. "I'm just drawn to stories that I can personally connect with."

Although she was still relatively inexperienced, Kristen now knew that she could carry a larger role. She knew how to behave like a pro, even when she was awestruck by supporting cast mates like the amazing Jodie Foster.

If there was ever a Kristen Stewart formula for success, it was this: Work with the best in the business and get better (much better!) as a result.

The first project Kristen pursued after *Panic Room* was another thriller with a very different setup than the first. Directed by Academy Award–nominated Mike Figgis, *Cold Creek Manor* stars Dennis Quaid and Sharon Stone as Cooper and Leah Tilson, a couple from New York City who move to the country with their son and daughter for a safer, calmer life.

Safer? Calmer? Ha! When the Tilsons purchase the enormous, falling-apart Cold Creek Manor mansion in the middle of nowhere, "safe" and "calm" are not the first words that come to mind. Instead, the family comes face-to-face with extreme danger. Dale, the former owner of the house, has just been released from jail. He befriends the Tilsons. Of course, it turns out the guy is a total psychopath.

Kristen plays the daughter, Kristen Tilson, (nice first name, eh?). Ryan Wilson plays her brother, Jesse. The two kids and their parents are snared in a serious game of cat-and-mouse with bad guy Dale. Kristen spends a lot of time running and screaming in this movie, which doesn't really give her a chance to show off *all* of her acting abilities, but it proves to be a wild ride nonetheless — complete with a swimming pool, a horse, and snakes — *lots* of snakes. She got to work with some great cast members, too, including the award-winning Quaid, Stone, and so-bad-he's-good villain, actor Stephen Dorff.

Although critics didn't love *Cold Creek Manor* (and, as it turned out, neither did audiences), Kristen's performance rang true. Directors and actors knew this girl was the real deal. Once again she was nominated for a Young Artist Award in the category of "Best Performance in a Feature Film — Supporting Young Actress" for *Cold Creek Manor.*

Everyone wanted to see what she'd do for her encore.

The next project for the now-twelve-year-old Kristen came quickly. She caught the attention of independent filmmaker Bart Freundlich, who was in the midst of developing a clever and funny remake of a Dutch movie called *Klatretøsen*. His Americanized version of the film, *Catch That Kid*, was about to go into production. He needed a relatively unknown, young leading actress with enough spunk, sass, and strength to climb big, big rocks and carry his motion picture.

Who better to do all those things than the spark plug who lit up the screen with Jodie Foster in *Panic Room*?

Freundlich knew Kristen was just right for the starring role of Maddy Phillips. Everything about Kristen's real-life persona exuded intelligence and wit. Those were exactly the qualities needed for the larger-than-life character of Maddy. Three cheers for Kristen Stewart! It marked her first "official" leading role.

Catch That Kid is part action-adventure, part drama, and part comedy — like *Spy Kids* meets *Mission: Impossible*. In the film, Kristen's dad sustains a life-threatening injury while rock climbing. His only hope is an experimental surgery that costs — *hold your breath!* — $250,000. That's a hefty quarter of a million dollars!

Super-desperate, Maddy tries to figure out where she can come up with that much cash. By booking back-to-back babysitting weekends? By auctioning off a collection of classic Barbies on eBay? Nope! There was only one way to get that much money fast.

Rob a bank!

Maddy hatches a sneaky plan to help her dad get the surgery he needs. In order to break into the bank, she enlists the help of two super-smart guy friends, played by Max Thieriot and Corbin Bleu (of *High School Musical* fame, before he was bopping and bouncing basketballs with Troy, aka heartthrob Zac Efron). Max plays Gus, a computer genius, and Corbin plays Austin, a mechanical genius who races go-carts. She convinces both boys to help her stage the heist at a super-locked-down bank.

Just why is the heist so dangerous? The bank vault hangs a frightening thirty feet in the air!

The *New York Times* review for *Catch That Kid* called the flick the "ultimate 'don't try this at home' movie." (That's true — *don't* try a heist at home, or anywhere for that matter!) But it gave Kristen her first real experience performing some serious stunt work. She loved it.

She told *Time for Kids* magazine: "I actually got to do a couple of weeks of training for climbing prior to the actual climbing of the water tower. I was on a crane so I wasn't technically climbing, but I had to get myself up there."

In addition to loving *Catch That Kid*'s action, Kristen also loved the movie's messages of loyalty and trust.

"I think [*Catch That Kid*] shows that if you have a best friend, you help them no matter what happens," Kristen explained to *Time for Kids*. "I think that it empowers kids and kids like that."

Although the movie was loads of fun to make and young audience members seemed to relate to the strong heroine of Maddy, *Catch That Kid* did not really catch the attention of its intended audience. Lukewarm reviews also hurt the film. It disappeared out of theaters almost immediately. But hit or not, *Catch That Kid* was still a huge stepping-stone in Kristen's career. It marked an important milestone on her résumé.

After *Catch That Kid*, Kristen decided to act in a unique thriller called *Undertow*. The movie, directed by David Gordon Green, starred teen actor Jamie Bell (best known for his performance in *Billy Elliot*) as a rough-around-the-edges boy named Chris. He appears alongside Hollywood hunks Josh Lucas (as his uncle, Deel) and Dermot Mulroney (as his father, John). *Undertow* traces the brotherhood between Deel and John — and how their angry, violent relationship changes the very course of young Chris's life.

Chris gets pulled under by the actions of his father and uncle, as if he has been dragged underwater by a *real* undertow. During all this, Kristen has a relatively

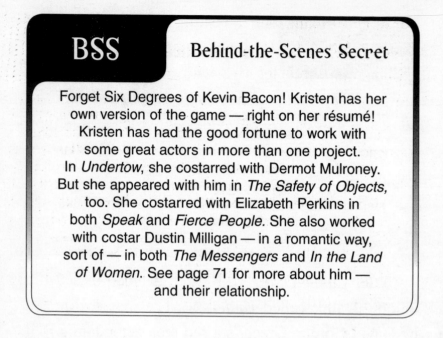

BSS · Behind-the-Scenes Secret

Forget Six Degrees of Kevin Bacon! Kristen has her own version of the game — right on her résumé! Kristen has had the good fortune to work with some great actors in more than one project. In *Undertow*, she costarred with Dermot Mulroney. But she appeared with him in *The Safety of Objects*, too. She costarred with Elizabeth Perkins in both *Speak* and *Fierce People.* She also worked with costar Dustin Milligan — in a romantic way, sort of — in both *The Messengers* and *In the Land of Women*. See page 71 for more about him — and their relationship.

minor role. She plays Lila, a young girlfriend to Chris who appears early in the film — and then ends their relationship.

Unfortunately for Kristen (and the other actors involved), *Undertow* got hardly any attention at all, and got almost no screen time in theaters. Yet despite the poor distribution of the film, Kristen got her share of attention for the project. Once again, Kristen was nominated for a Young Artist Award in the category of

"Best Performance in a Feature Film — Supporting Young Actress" for *Undertow*.

She was three for five with award noms for her movies! That is quite an accomplishment. Although not all of the movies she was choosing to act in were performing well at the box office, somehow Kristen was still getting the attention she deserved.

All Kristen needed now was a little bit of luck and perfect timing.

But could she find the right movie to showcase her talent *and* get her to the next level of stardom?

You go, girl!

Chapter 4

Speak Up! The Start of Something Big

"I like being in movies that tell a great story."

That's what Kristen told Australia's girlfriend.com website during one interview. So when the opportunity came along to star in the movie *Speak*, directed by Jessica Sharzer, Kristen jumped at it.

Speak tells a great, although difficult, story.

The movie is adapted from the best-selling novel by Laurie Halse Anderson. *Speak* is about a young girl named Melinda Sordino, who decides to stop almost all verbal contact with her friends and family after she is attacked by an upperclassman at a school party.

Kristen was only thirteen years old when she played the part of Melinda, but she handled the complexities of the *Speak* role with the skill of a more experienced actress. It was a tough part: The character of Melinda is the lead role, yet she has very few speaking lines of dialogue. Instead, there is a running narration of Melinda's thoughts and commentary. As Melinda, Kristen did a lot of her most powerful acting with her body, mouth, and eyes.

As the movie progresses, Melinda faces one challenge after the next. She tries to forge a friendship with a new girl, but cannot face the cliques and queen bees that go along with that relationship. She keeps running into the boy who assaulted her (more than once) in the hallways at school. She deals with distant parents and insufferable teachers (including one called Mr. Neck!).

In the midst of all this inner (and outer) chaos, Melinda finds a few places of peace. She discovers a secret storage room at school where she goes to express herself. She also meets a hip, new art teacher (played by funny guy/actor Steve Zahn) with the too-cool and oh-so-appropriate name Mr. Freeman. Mr. Freeman helps Melinda to escape the pain she has been carting around. He helps her learn how to draw, to restore the confidence she lost a year earlier after the disastrous party incident, and to speak again.

Kristen portrays the transformation — and catharsis — of the character Melinda. At first, Melinda appears to be just another misfit, alienated and shunned (one kid calls her "the most depressed person I've ever known"). She has clueless, self-absorbed parents and she has lost her girlfriends. The movie balances flash-backs of Melinda's traumatic event as she deals with its aftermath so it is really two stories, past and present, working at the same time.

Speak wowed audiences, mostly due to the perfor-mance of its leading lady. The praise for Kristen's performance was overwhelming.

Movie City News, from Sundance, said, "Ms. Stewart is her own unique individual . . . her energy is cobra-like and . . . as an actor, she is not a victim. Not ever. Not even when she is being victimized. . . . She can burn a hole in you with her stare. And she can make you want to work to help her when her eyes tell you she's lost."

An efilmcritic.com reviewer wrote, "The teen star of *Panic Room* and *Cold Creek Manor* shows that she's far more than just a 'teen actress,' delivering a flawless performance."

One of the biggest fans of the film — and of Kristen Stewart's performance — was the original book's author, Laurie Halse Anderson. In an interview with teenreads.com, Anderson said, "Kristen Stewart's acting is fantastic. I think her facial expressions speak volumes."

Most critics recognized that Kristen's acting was special because she avoided falling into any dramatic traps in the role of Melinda. She very easily could have played the sullen, sad girl without humor. But she didn't. Melinda's interior monologues throughout the film teem with Kristen's dark, biting sense of humor. She is able to play both a dark and light character at the same time.

BSS   Behind-the-Scenes Secret

During the filming of *Speak*, something important happened to Kristen Stewart *off* camera. She fell for one of her costars. Michael Angarano played her science lab partner in the movie. The two had great chemistry on screen — and off. Kristen recently told *Vanity Fair* magazine that her secret boy crush is actually no secret at all: It's "my boyfriend, Michael Angarano." And to think it all started with this movie! For more info about Michael and some of Kristen's other friends (and costars) who just happen to be boys, turn to page 68.

Once again, *Speak* was a film packed with star power. In addition to actor Steve Zahn (*Daddy Day Care*), Kristen costarred with actress Elizabeth Perkins as her mother and actor D.B. Sweeney as her father. (Perkins is maybe best known for her role as the girlfriend/co-worker in the Tom Hanks smash, *Big*.)

The role of Melinda in *Speak* came at an especially interesting time in Kristen's life. Although she had won praise for her maturity and acting ability, Kristen faced some of the same adolescent problems — and insecurities — that the character Melinda did. When acting in the role, Kristen may have seemed so much older than her thirteen years, but in reality, Kristen was just a tween, too! At the time when *Speak* was filmed, she was going through a lot of her own real-life changes.

In an interview with *Teen Hollywood*, Kristen remembered the time when she was younger, around the age just before she made *Speak*. "I didn't have any inhibitions, I wasn't embarrassed about doing anything. When you get older, I don't know what it is, it's not that you get more insecure, you're just maybe more self-aware. It's just kind of something that happens."

It was definitely happening to her.

"When I was little," Kristen told *Cosmo Girl* magazine in 2007, "I was so confident and comfortable in my own skin, I would say anything to anyone. Then you turn thirteen . . . you're really inhibited and insecure."

Was Kristen able to show a deeper vulnerability on screen because of her adolescence and everything else going on in her real life? Do Kristen and the character of Melinda share the same desires to break out and speak up?

Disappointingly, *Speak* did not deliver at the box office. Despite heaps of critical praise and an amazing cast, no one even gave *Speak* a feature film distribution deal! Instead, *Speak* debuted on Showtime and then later on Lifetime television in an edited form. Although it got good reviews and a strong television audience, Kristen's best performance to date got a little lost between the cracks.

If Kristen was worried about it, however, she didn't show it. At every stage, Kristen has been comfortable with the progress of her career and the choices she has made. So many young actors and actresses have a need to make it "big." Sometimes fame hits before the actors even have a chance to come to terms with their own talents and desires. Kristen seemed to know that taking her time meant a chance to explore, to fall down, and to make mistakes as an actor. She was able to take more time getting to know her craft — and herself.

Author A. M. Homes (*The Safety of Objects*) considered Kristen's experiences as a path to growing up — with both good and bad elements. Homes observed in an interview with Kristen for *Interview* magazine, "Call it what you will — talent, grace, *joie de vivre* — but whatever it is, Kristen Stewart comes off as one-hundred percent natural. Entirely absent of affectation, she could be almost any kid growing up in California, except that she's growing up to be a movie star."

When *Speak* was not picked up for theatrical distribution, Kristen did not let the lack of exposure for the movie — or for herself — get in the way. She did not worry about achieving a level of stardom where many expected she *should* be.

Right now, she prefers anonymity.

"[I'm] really lucky," she told *Justine* magazine. "But as rewarding and fulfilling as the work is, it [still] doesn't really — feel like anything. I still go home every day to the same people and we just sit at the dinner table and trip out a little bit about what's going on."

If there is such a thing as a Hollywood machine, Kristen does not seem to be getting sucked up into it. She comes from a showbiz family, but she remains close to her parents and brothers. She decided to be home-schooled from the eighth grade onward, which gives her greater flexibility when she works and travels for her job. If anything, Kristen made a decision to learn — and do — more than ever before.

"If there is anything you really want to do, you have to give it a shot," Kristen told *Teen Ink* magazine, referring to her acting and show business ambitions. "Otherwise you're going to hold on to it forever and just regret it.

"You should have no regret."

Chapter 5

Another Fantastic Journey: Making *Zathura*

Jon Favreau described Kristen Stewart perfectly in *Interview* magazine.

"You really stood out as having a presence, and a look, and chops, and poise," he complimented her. "Most young girls or boys have sort of an unfocused, scattered energy. You have a very still energy to you."

So was it an admirable ability to be "still" that got Kristen the part in Jon's film *Zathura*? After all, she spends half the movie frozen.

There were numerous reasons why Kristen seemed to fit right in with the material, including her connection with the director and her desire to "do something different" with her acting. *Zathura* was a broad comedy with a science fiction twist. Laughing had not typically been a part of Kristen's job description, but she wanted to give it a try.

The movie *Zathura* is a followup to the book and popular movie *Jumanji*, but the two are not written as partners. Both were original picture books written and illustrated by famous kid's author and artist Chris van Allsburg. He's the same guy who created *The Polar Express*.

Zathura is a space fantasy. Two young brothers, six-year-old Danny (played by Jonah Bobo) and ten-year-old Walter (played by Josh Hutcherson), are busy arguing *again*, as most brothers do. But when they find an old board game called *Zathura* in their house, they start playing and — surprise! — they finally stop arguing. In fact, they stop doing anything normal. Playing the game turns their suburban house into a spaceship hurtling through space, somewhere in the vicinity of Saturn.

Whoops.

Kristen plays the boys' big sister Lisa. Once the boys realize that they have somehow sent their house into orbit, they wake up Lisa and tell her what's happening. Big surprise: She doesn't believe them at first.

Lisa is the doubting, crabby older sister who wants the boys to just leave her alone!

Kristen told TeenHollywood.com, "[This] was my first comedy, so I had a lot of anticipation and apprehension as to how I was going to react to situations that are over the top and hokey and hysterical. I was too embarrassed to explore the scenes and be free with them. [Director Jon Favreau] helped me to push past my inhibitions because he was very in tune to how his actors were feeling."

As the game (and the movie) progress (and Lisa finally realizes that the game is *really* happening), the house begins to spin and wobble through space, getting whacked by meteors. When a bunch of creepy reptilian creatures called Zorgons climb aboard the house, Lisa's bathroom turns into a quick-freezer.

Whoops — again.

Lisa (aka Kristen) becomes a rigid, frost-covered ice sculpture for the rest of the movie. Will Danny and Walter escape from gravitational forces that are pulling the house (and them) into some strange space void? What happens to Lisa now that she has turned into a human ice cube?

If the movie sounds "out there," it is. But Kristen

admits that despite the frozen bathroom, she had an ice, er . . . *nice* time playing around with the film's special effects.

She didn't mind dealing with lots of on-set monsters — or goofy, murderous robots — one bit. She liked the experience of doing harness work in which she got to "fly." And the full body cast was . . . *fun*?

She explained the complex process to Teenhollywood.com.

"It was pretty arduous . . . a three-step process. The first was a digital scan of my body that they entered into a computer. [Then] they molded, individually, each part of my body . . . my legs, my torso, each one of my arms, my head. The head was a bit of a worry. I'm pretty claustrophobic and it gets really heavy and the plaster is warm so you can't even feel the air go into your nose because it's warm. I mean you're breathing but it's kind of scary. The last step in the process was painting. I went in and stood next to my mannequin . . . [while] they painted every nuance of my face. Every freckle on my arm is on that body."

One of the weirdest things about having a complete body cast painted to look *exactly* like you: the twin factor. "It's surreal," Kristen explained. "It's an experience that no human being has ever really done unless they have a twin: standing next to themselves."

Of course, the plaster model wasn't actually a perfect twin. The cryogenically frozen (which means frozen at *very* low temperatures) Lisa had blue, frozen lips and frosted hair. It's a good look if you're hanging with Frosty the Snowman!

Kristen loved all the special effects. Most were not CGI (computer generated images), so when there were fireballs or lizard men — it was all right there, up close and personal.

"It wasn't like watching a video game," Kristen explained to TeenHollywood.com. "We never had to run away from the imaginary robot. We never had to run away from the guy in the green suit. They were real characters. . . . They actually made little mechanical muscles underneath the rubber of their skin."

Eventually, the boys realize that the only way they can win the game of *Zathura* is to finish it. And the only way to finish it is to cooperate with one another. (Otherwise their lovely sister Lisa may stay frozen forever!)

In the end, *Zathura* may be a space fantasy, but it is really about getting along with your siblings. Kristen

There was almost no green screen used in the making of this movie! When the kids harpooned walls on set — they really shot harpoons. When there was a fire, Kristen really used a fire extinguisher to put it out on screen. There were three different house sets used. The boys (and Kristen) had fun destroying at least two of them!

liked that part of the movie's message a lot, especially since she is so close to her own brothers and parents.

Going into the production of *Zathura,* Kristen wanted to gain some new experiences. Although making the full body cast was definitely one of the most unique, another thing she got from the movie was the opportunity to really "get" comedy.

Kristen has been labeled an intense and serious actress in many of her films so far. So what did she learn most of all from acting in *Zathura*?

How to have fun!

"Comedy is kind of a serious business, you know. It's all about timing," Kristen explained to TeenHollywood.com. "But it's not that big of a deal. [I have to] go with it."

Kristen had one adult costar in the film: comedian Dax Shepard. He plays an astronaut lost in the game. The kids encounter him while flying through space. Dax tried to give Kristen his best advice about playing comedy: "Don't think so hard. It'll show up on screen if you are having fun," he told her.

Dax was right. In one funny scene, Kristen appears transfixed by his stare and just like that, her tough edges fade away. She falls for him as if she's under a spell.

It is fun to watch Kristen switch acting gears from freaked out to fearlessly devoted. And by the end of the movie, of course, Kristen gets back to her snippy self. She makes her brothers promise they will *never* mention what happened in space.

On the career checklist, *Zathura* gave Kristen the chance to check off yet one more movie genre she had not yet tried. She was racking up serious skills for a young actress! Kristen could play super-serious. She could scream her lungs out. Now she could just let go and be funny.

Best of all, Kristen Jaymes Stewart could survive a deadly deep freeze!

You can't get much cooler than that.

Chapter 6

Taking Risks: *Fierce People* and *The Messengers*

Perhaps what makes Kristen cool — and continues to set her apart from her peers — is her choice of roles.

Kristen has a willingness to take unusual and not always pretty parts.

While other tween actresses are starring in *High School Musical* or sweet romantic comedies, Kristen takes parts in more serious films. Hey, even the "comedy" *Zathura* had its serious undertones. You can't have murdering robots and attacking Zorgons and not call that a little bit *serious*, right?

By choosing the more intense, less traditional parts, Kristen continues to follow the path that her screen idol Jodie Foster blazed before her.

Unfortunately, following a path like that can be risky. Challenging movies come with their own problems. For starters, they have less commercial appeal. That means that a person can do the best acting job in the world but no one might see — or like — or even *get* — the movie.

Fierce People was one of those projects. Although the movie found a small legion of fans, it opened and closed in U.S. theaters in the blink of an eye — going right to DVD.

On the surface, *Fierce People* seemed like a dream project. The cast included legendary actor Donald Sutherland, actress Diane Lane, teen hottie Chris Evans, Elizabeth Perkins (who, as you may recall, played Kristen's mother in *Speak),* and Anton Yelchin, a young actor in his first major leading role. It was directed by Griffin Dunne, himself the son of a "royal" Hollywood family of writers and actors.

What could be better than that?

In the movie, Anton plays sixteen-year-old Finn, a boy stuck in a dead end situation with his mom, Liz, a massage therapist played by Diane Lane. Dad's off in Africa somewhere. Mom Liz is in "recovery." Desperate to give her son a decent summer, she moves the two of them out of their lousy city apartment to a sprawling (9,856 acres!) mansion in the country. The too-rich owner of the manor is Sutherland, in the role of Ogden Osbourne. He's a zillionaire, but he also happens to be one of Liz's clients. Although the plot is a little complicated, Finn and Liz seem okay at the mansion — at first. Finn and Osbourne's grandkids are getting along.

Kristen plays Osbourne's granddaughter Maya. She falls for Finn. But this was no ordinary romantic role for Kristen. (Nothing is really ordinary about this movie!)

Director Dunne was blown away by Kristen's maturity for such a young actress. At the time of filming, she was only fourteen! He thought she was a lot closer to eighteen, a mistake many people make when they see Kristen on screen. So how was he able to shoot a romantic scene between the two young actors?

Very carefully.

Thanks to strict labor laws, kids can only work a certain number of hours each day, based on their ages. (That's why very young stars/babies are often played by twins, so one can come into a scene when the other one gets tired or has been working for a set amount of time.) Laws also prohibit showing certain things on camera, like skin. Kristen was not allowed — or interested — in any body-revealing scenes.

Dunne told Aboutfilm.com, "I was always going to be really careful with the age and how I was going to shoot it. [But] both Anton's and Kristen's parents were comfortable. I only had forty-five minutes to do the whole thing. I know if I had kids who were eighteen playing younger . . . it would have been much more revealing. The restraints really helped me."

For Kristen, the most positive thing about filming *Fierce People* was, in fact, the people. Actress Diane Lane, like Jodie Foster, has been working in movies since she was very young. In the late 1970s, she co-starred in a classic romance movie for kids, *A Little Romance* (which, by the way, is still a must-see!). She knew a lot about filming awkward scenes and working with great actors (in *A Little Romance*, she acted with the great Sir Laurence Olivier, who is known as one of the best actors *ever*!). Diane was on hand to offer wisdom from her experiences to Kristen.

"What drew [Diane] to this role, and the presence

she was on this set with Anton and Kristen," director Dunne told Aboutmovies.com, "was that she was very much an aware and protective mother. It was very maternal, and the kids took advantage."

After filming *Fierce People*, Kristen landed a huge role! She was picked to star in a brand-new Hollywood thriller called *The Messengers*, directed by the Pang Brothers. Danny and Oxide Pang are a team of twin directors who had just made a knockout Asian horror flick called *The Eye* (the 2008 remake starred Jessica Alba). Kristen was a big fan of the movie.

Of all the types of movies that Kristen has made, thrillers are at the top of the list. First, there was *Panic Room;* then *Cold Creek Manor*. Now Kristen's new movie, *The Messengers*, gave her an all-new reason to scream.

Asian horror films have been a popular genre since the turn of the millennium. Hugely popular movies like *The Ring* and *The Grudge* were adapted from Asian movies for American audiences. Both starred famous, non-Asian actresses in the lead roles, too: Naomi Watts for *The Ring* and *The Ring 2*, and Sarah Michelle

Kristen joins some impressive company with her "screaming" role in *The Messengers*. Scores of other actresses lent their loud lung power to horror movies of the past. There are legions of teens who screamed their way through horror classics, like Jamie Lee Curtis (inside the closet in the original *Halloween*); Sarah Michelle Gellar (letting out a wail inside the weird house in *The Grudge*), and Neve Campbell (in the oh-so-perfectly-named *Scream*)!

Gellar for *The Grudge* (and about two seconds in *The Grudge 2*).

What makes an Asian horror film stand apart from typical scary fare at the multiplex?

Kristen has a theory. She told Moviesonline.com, "[Asian films are] not as heavy-handed as American films. They tend to take their time a little bit and let you think for yourself before they hammer you in the face and smash people's brains in and drag them off into the woods . . . I think they're smarter. I mean, not to generalize about stuff like that but . . . I like their slow deliberateness."

It sounds weird, but horror flicks make Kristen happy.

"I like when all of a sudden you're watching a movie and it slows down and you're like, 'Oh . . . something's definitely going to happen' and you know it, but even when it does, it still scares you just as much."

In *The Messengers,* Kristen plays sixteen-year-old Jess Solomon. Her family (Dad, Mom, and three-year-old baby brother) have left big-city life for a secluded farm in North Dakota. Soon after they arrive at their new home, Jess and her brother begin seeing ominous apparitions that no one else can see.

Jess and her little brother are repeatedly attacked by something from the other side. In one scene, Jess gets weird scratches on her neck. In another scene, she's nearly swallowed up by her basement floor. No spoilers here, though! You'll have to see the movie for yourself to find out what's making all those ghosts so mad. . . .

Kristen loved the unusual setting of *The Messengers* — a giant sunflower farm. But the set was anything but sunny. Although the landscape was wide open, there was an isolating, creepy vibe.

"It's a classically American setting . . . a beautiful sunflower farm . . . and at the same time these really

Does the real Kristen Stewart believe in ghosts and paranormal stuff?

"Ever since I've been a kid, I've been absolutely, totally scared of ghosts. Like whenever I would run around my house terrified when I was five years old, it was always because of ghosts," Kristen told Moviesonline.com. "But I definitely haven't been inclined to sit down and type 'ghost' into Google." Then, Kristen shared a super scary ghost experience. "Halfway through [the film], I had a really trippy experience in my hotel room," Kristen explained. "It was an old hotel. One night, it was insane, I opened my eyes and this image of this woman just filled my entire view . . . I let out the most gut-wrenching scream. People called the hotel room to see if I was okay."

incredibly terrifying, threatening events are taking place every single day that this girl is there," she told Moviesonline.com. "Most of our horror sequences are in the basement and the cellar and the house is dark itself."

Kristen spends most of the film (and most of her acting energy) trying to convince Mom and Dad that she is telling the truth about the ghosts. She also spends a lot of time evading those mysterious ghosts all over (and under) her house. It was harder work than she ever expected. "I am catatonically terrified . . . most of the time," she told Teenhollywood.com.

"I thought doing this would be a nice break. I could just go and do this little horror movie . . . but it was one of the hardest jobs I've ever taken on!" she confessed to *Total Sci Fi* magazine. "It was just physically strenuous having the same expression in so many frames. [There's] scary face one, scary face two . . . For two weeks straight I was just screaming and just acting terrified."

The movie, like so many other movies in Kristen's impressive résumé, starred some big-name actors: Dylan McDermott and Penelope Ann Miller play Dad and Mom; John Corbett plays a creepy dude who lives nearby; and teen Dustin Milligan plays a boy from town who befriends Jess. But, despite the talented cast (combined with Kristen's talent!), *The Messengers* did not win any awards and did not deliver at the box office. The movie was panned by critics.

Yeowch.

Once again, however, Kristen's experiences added

up to more than the sum of their parts. She did not need starred reviews from all the major magazines to make her feel good about her performance. And just because the film wasn't a smash hit, she didn't consider it a failure.

Over time, by taking risky roles in movies like *Fierce People* or *The Messengers*, Kristen was learning wise lessons about the business of movies. These lessons were reinforced by her parents, based on their own years in the business.

Lesson One: There is no such thing as a sure thing.

Lesson Two: Don't underestimate the challenges of the job.

Lesson Three: There's always a new project!

Before *The Messengers* was out, Kristen was already on to her next movie. This time, she was cast in a drama with a little bit of romance . . . and one of the cutest actors from TV.

Chapter 7

Finding Her Way:
In the Land of Women — and Beyond

If "cool" were a subject in school, Kristen Jaymes Stewart would be getting an A+. Her ability to choose movies that make her a better actress is as impressive as the lineup of actors and actresses who served as her mentors on each of those projects.

So far, Kristen's career hasn't been about starring in hits. Instead, it's about hitting the stars. Kristen aims high in all that she does. She considers her journey as an actress one of the greatest educations a person can get.

Around the seventh grade, Kristen (and her parents) made the choice to leave public school. She wanted to focus on her acting. She enrolled at Laurel Springs Distance Learning School, based in Ojai, California. This way she could pursue her acting career *and* continue her education at the same time.

Long-distance learning provides an online teacher for each student, follows state standards, and delivers transcripts and diplomas. Other kids who attend (or attended) Laurel Springs include actresses Hayden Panettiere, Raven-Symoné (from *That's So Raven*), Jennifer Love Hewitt (from *Ghost Whisperer*), and Dakota Fanning (*Charlotte's Web*); *American Idol* winner Jordin Sparks; and Olympic silver medal, pairs figure skater Tanith Belbin.

BSS Behind-the-Scenes Secret

Many actresses (and athletes, singers, and other kids) have been tutored on sets or while touring during high school years. They then went on to college and higher education in a more traditional way. Jodie Foster did it at Yale University — graduating magna cum laude (that means with high honors) with a degree in literature! Actresses like Maggie Gyllenhaal, Julia Stiles, and others also got Ivy League degrees while continuing to act. Natalie Portman got a degree in psychology from Harvard! Kristen wants to do the same kind of thing. Other college all-stars: Before hitting it big Ashton Kutcher was a biochemical engineering major at the University of Iowa . . . Gwyneth Paltrow studied art history at UC Santa Barbara . . . and Brad Pitt studied journalism at the University of Missouri.

After experimenting with comedy, thrillers, and independent dramas, Kristen geared up for the next movie in her education. Although she'd played a few romantic scenes in movies like *Undertow,* romance was never really the focus for any of her characters.

But now she had been cast in *In the Land of Women,* directed by Jonathan Kasdan. Right off the bat, Kristen knew the movie would bring about some big changes. It was a transitional moment in her life — and this role reflected that.

BSS Behind-the-Scenes Secret

At the time when she was cast in *In the Land of Women,* Kristen had just filmed a short movie with Kate Hudson called *Cutlass.* The flick was filmed for a *Glamour* magazine promotion and contest. In it, Kristen plays a younger version of actress Virginia Madsen's character. She's a girl who wants a brand-new car. Because Madsen is a blond, Kristen had to dye her own long brown locks blond so they could look alike. Since she got a lot of compliments on the look, Kristen kept her hair blond for her new role in *In the Land of Women.* It made her look even more like actress Meg Ryan's daughter!

Panic Room

Red Carpet Glam

Meet the Press

Kristen Stewart

Kristen Stewart

Into the Wild

Zathura

As *In the Land of Women* opens, we meet Carter Webb, the leading man played by TV heartthrob Adam Brody. At the time of the movie's filming and release, he was starring in a super-popular teen show called *The O.C.*

Poor Carter! He's just been dumped by his starlet girlfriend, so he goes off to live in Michigan with his grandmother (played by Oscar winner Olympia Dukakis). She's the first woman we meet in the title's "Land of Women." It turns out his grandmother is neighbors with a few other women, too. Soon Carter gets involved with them: Makenzie Vega, who plays Paige Hardwicke; Kristen, who plays Lucy Hardwicke; and Meg Ryan, who plays the mom of the two girls.

"It's a really nice, bold, coming-of-age story," Kristen told *Justine* magazine. "I [could relate to the character]. I definitely felt that when I turned sixteen, I kind of came out of it, too."

"Basically, [*In the Land of Women*] is about people talking to people," Kristen said during an interview with TeenHollywood.com. "I'm the daughter with the typical problems with her mother and the typical problems of high school and growing up and insecurities. Through talking to this guy, she kind of realizes a lot about herself, what type of direction she'd like her life to go in."

Talk about life lessons! Kristen has a lot to say about the things she has gone through as a teenager — things that may or may not be the same as things experienced by her character Lucy (or the characters in any of her films). Despite her untraditional upbringing, and lack of public school experience, Kristen Stewart really "gets" it.

"[*In the Land of Women* shows a] really typical relationship where you don't quite know why but you're not getting along with your mom. You just don't want to share certain things with her, and there's a resentment. You don't necessarily believe that (your mom) is there for you — it's sort of fake," she told *Justine* magazine. "I've never had any weird problems with (my parents), but I totally see Lucy in a lot of my friends."

Kristen believes she avoided a lot of the adolescent pitfalls and drama in her life because she avoided public school after eighth grade. By doing that, she didn't have to face the enormous pressure of grades, cliques, popularity, and boys in the same way that many of her non-actor friends did. (Of course, she had to deal with seventeen-hour days shooting a horror movie in Canada with a bunch of crazy black crows, but who's keeping score — ha!)

Although she does not share Lucy's problems in real life, Kristen is somehow able to show that teen angst and desire. She makes us believe her experience one hundred percent. That's what you call being a good — no, a *great* — actress!

In *Interview* magazine, Kristen confided in her interviewer Jon Favreau (who not only directed her in *Zathura* but who she calls a good friend). She shared a little bit about how she feels living her teen years on a movie set. Their conversation reveals the truth about sacrifices — and shifts — that a young actor faces when he or she chooses a different path than a "normal" teenager.

Jon Favreau: Are you able to maintain friendships with people you went to school with?

Kristen Stewart: When I stopped going to school, I got the strongest dose of perspective. When you're a kid, your friends, your school, your teachers, your family — that's your whole world, your whole existence. When I stopped going, I lost all my friends but the few that were really close to me.

On the set of *In the Land of Women*, Kristen learned a lot about love.

"With Carter, [Lucy] gets her first sense of puppy love even though he's way too old for her. At first she has romantic expectations, but it's more that she's lost and here's this guy who is there for her and he listens to her," Kristen said to VisualHollywood.com. "Carter teaches Lucy a valuable lesson . . . you can't allow your fears and resentments to inhibit your life."

What really makes an on-screen high school romance *waaay* better than the offscreen kind?
We can think of three reasons right off the bat (and Kristen would *have* to agree . . .)

1. You can always reshoot a movie scene if things don't go quite right.

2. On set, someone is there to feed you all the good lines so there's never that "Did I really say that?" moment.

3. You get to date the captain of the football team (like Lucy does in *In the Land of Women*), dump him, and then fall for the cute boy who works at Orange Julius at the mall (like Lucy does in the movie) — without any fear of social exile. In other words, in movie high school you can do whatever you want and get your happily-ever-after ending.

Bonus: You also get hair, makeup, *and* your pick from the wardrobe closet. Sweet!

Chapter 8

I Stilll ♥ My Job: Boys, Boys, and More Boys

In *In the Land of Women,* Kristen shared her first major on-screen kiss. She mashed with Adam Brody's character Carter. Surely, there must have been some butterflies inside when they locked lips.

Kristen told *Girls' Life* magazine, "There are different degrees of real kissing. I'm so concerned with what I look like during kissing scenes . . . I have to get over it." As usual, she makes the making-of-a-romance-movie sound like all business.

The truth is that no matter what Kristen thinks about kissing boys on screen (or off), she knows a lot about the opposite sex. For starters, she's super-close to the main "boy" in her life: dear, sweet Dad. John Stewart has been one of Kristen's biggest fans and influences from the very start of her career. Dad is always watching over her.

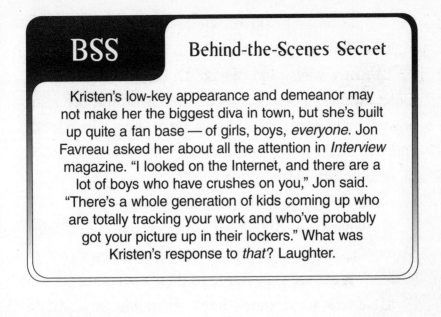

Kristen's low-key appearance and demeanor may not make her the biggest diva in town, but she's built up quite a fan base — of girls, boys, *everyone*. Jon Favreau asked her about all the attention in *Interview* magazine. "I looked on the Internet, and there are a lot of boys who have crushes on you," Jon said. "There's a whole generation of kids coming up who are totally tracking your work and who've probably got your picture up in their lockers." What was Kristen's response to *that*? Laughter.

Then there is Kristen's brother Cameron, a movie grip.

Kristen joked about growing up as the baby of the family during an interview with TeenHollywood.com: "I was tortured when I was little. I would sit in my brother's doorway because I really wanted to hang out with him really bad but I wasn't allowed in his room. . . . I'm a little sister."

One time Kristen got into *real* trouble with her brother. She and her brother were both racing for the telephone. He got it first — and then swung his arm out to hit Kristen with the phone. When he did that . . . he broke his arm! She had to spend the entire night in the emergency room with him.

In many ways (and maybe it's from living with all those brothers!) Kristen seems like a little more tomboy than a girly-girl. Sure, she's got gorgeous long locks and a model-pretty face, but this actress is so much more comfortable hanging around in a T-shirt and a pair of Levi's — just like one of the boys!

So what's the 411 about some of the cute hunks, nerds, and other guys who have been Kristen's costars to date? What are *they* doing in their own careers?

Here are some quick bites about the boys, boys, boys who have starred in the real-life story (and the many movies) of Kristen Stewart.

Crush time!

Name: Dustin Milligan

Born: July 28, 1985, in Yellowknife, Northwest
Territories (Canada)

Tall Factor: 5' 10 1/2"

Why You Know Him: Starring in the new 90210 on TV
as jock Ethan Ward

Other Roles: In the Land of Women, The Butterfly
Effect 2, Final Destination 3

Fun Facts: His favorite cereal is called Shreddies (from
Canada); he started a scholarship for kids at
his former high school, École Sir John Franklin
High School. It's called the Enough Talk, Hurry
Up and Do It Already Arts Scholarship Fund, to
help graduates study drama or the arts.

Kristen Connection: In the Land of Women and
The Messengers

Real-Life Love!

Name: Michael Angarano

Born: December 3, 1987, in Brooklyn, New York

Tall Factor: 5' 7"

Why You Know Him: Played Jack's son Elliott on *Will & Grace* (TV) and Meryl Streep's student in *Music of the Heart* (he learned the violin for the role!)

Other Roles: *Almost Famous, Lords of Dogtown, Sky High*

Fun Facts: He was one of three finalists for the role of Anakin Skywalker in *Star Wars: The Phantom Menace*; he wants to go to film school at University of Southern California (USC)

Kristen Connection: Kristen is his girlfriend!

Name: Corbin Bleu

Born: February 21, 1989, in Brooklyn, New York

Tall Factor: 5' 9"

Why You Know Him: *High School Musical* and its
 sequels, playing Troy (Zac Efron's)
 buddy Chad

Other Roles: *Catch That Kid, Jump In, Flight
 29 Down*

Fun Facts: He was a model as a kid for places
 like Target and Toys "R" Us; his favorite
 school subject was science.

Kristen Connection: Starred together in
 Catch That Kid

Name: Anton Yelchin

Born: March 11, 1989, in Leningrad, USSR

(now Saint Petersburg, Russia)

Tall Factor: 5' 9"

Why You Know Him: Won a Young Artist Award in

2002 for Hearts in Atlantis

Other Roles: Charlie Bartlett, House of D, and the

soon-to-come new Star Trek (playing Pavel

Chekov)

Fun Facts: His parents were both professional figure

skaters who immigrated to the United States

when he was only six months old; he plays piano

and guitar in a band; he also plays chess.

Kristen Connection: Starred in Fierce People

Name: Adam Brody

Born: December 15, 1979, in San Diego, California (where he pretty much lived at the beach)

Tall Factor: 5' 11"

Why You Know Him: Starring as Seth Cohen on the TV show *The O.C.*

Other Roles: *Mr. and Mrs. Smith* (with Angelina Jolie and Brad Pitt!)

Fun Facts: He was the first guy actor ever on the cover of *Elle Girl* magazine; he plays drums for a band called Big Japan; he co-wrote a comic book miniseries called the Red Menace.

Kristen Connection: Appeared together in *In the Land of Women*

Name: Eddie Redmayne

Born: January 6, 1982, in London, England

Tall Factor: 5' 11"

Why You Know Him: Has had a lot of success with his stage career — and got his first U.S. break with a role in *The Good Shepherd*

Other Roles: *The Other Boleyn Girl*

Fun Facts: He went to Eton College and he studied history at Trinity College, Cambridge; he is also a model for Burberry.

Kristen Connection: Appeared together in *The Yellow Handkerchief*

On-screen Only!

Name: Jamie Bell

Born: March 14, 1986, in Stockton on Tees, England

Tall Factor: 5' 7"

Why You Know Him: Chosen from 2,000 kids in an open call to win the role of *Billy Elliot* in 1999, which won him numerous awards including England's prestigious BAFTA Best Actor award

Other Roles: *Jumper, Mister Foe, King Kong*

Fun Facts: He danced from a young age and his grandmother, mother, aunt, and sister were also dancers

Kristen Connection: Appeared in *Undertow* together

Name: Emile Hirsch

Born: March 13, 1985, grew up in Topanga, California

Tall Factor: 5' 7"

Why You Know Him: Starring role in 2002 film
The Dangerous Lives of Altar Boys

Other Roles: Lords of Dogtown (for which he trained
seriously in surfing and skateboarding for three
months!), Speed Racer

Fun Facts: His mother is a visual artist and pop-up
book designer; has been acting since age eight;
likes rapping and poetry; his costars in Speed
Racer were Kensey and Willy, two chimps who
played his monkey pal Chim-Chim.

Kristen Connection: Appeared together in Into the
Wild

On-screen Only!

Name: Ryan Reynolds

Born: October 23, 1976, in Vancouver,
British Columbia, Canada

Tall Factor: 6' 2"

Why You Know Him: *National Lampoon's Van Wilder* (he played the title character)

Other Roles: Starred in *Two Guys, a Girl, and a Pizza Place* on TV, *Definitely Maybe*

Fun Facts: He flunked his drama class in high school; has huge fear of flying because once he was skydiving and his parachute did not open immediately (luckily it eventually did!); he is one of four brothers

Kristen Connection: Appears in *Adventureland*

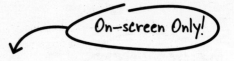

Name: Robert Pattinson

Born: May 13, 1986, in London, England

Tall Factor: 6' 1"

Why You Know Him: Cedric Diggory in Harry Potter
    and the Goblet of Fire

Other Roles: Vanity Fair (with Reese Witherspoon),
    Harry Potter and the Order of the Phoenix

Fun Facts: Rob (his nickname) started acting at age
    six, but only took it seriously when he real-
    ized that the local drama club (Barnes The-
    ater Company) was where he could find all the
    pretty girls! His favorite actor? Jack Nichol-
    son! "I used to try and be him . . . when I was
    thirteen, I [even] dressed like him!"

Kristen Connection: Twilight (of course!)

Chapter 9

A Natural Ability: *Into the Wild*

When Kristen first heard about the audition for a new movie called *Into the Wild,* she freaked out. Not only did she have to meet face-to-face with Oscar winner and director Sean Penn for a *private* audition — in addition to reading lines, Kristen would have to sing a song! Once again, Kristen was breaking new ground in her career.

Into the Wild was a passion project for director Penn. The film is based on the bestselling book by acclaimed author Jon Krakauer. It's the story of Christopher McCandless, a college grad who decided to give away his life savings, burn his ID, and hitch-hike to Alaska. Chris was obsessed with writers like Henry David Thoreau and Jack London, who wanted to abandon society and return to nature. Along the way, he met various people, including hippies, a farmer, and a leather worker. He did make it to Alaska and for a while was able to "live off the land." But in the end, he got trapped in the wilderness and died. It's a tragic ending.

In the movie, Chris McCandless is played by young actor Emile Hirsch (*Speed Racer*). Kristen plays a sensitive singer-songwriter who runs into Chris at one stop on his journey. Although her screen time is relatively short, Kristen's role is an important one. In its review of the film, the *Chicago Tribune* said that Kristen performed "vividly well with a sketch of a role."

During the auditioning process, Kristen had a serious case of butterflies. And why not? The first time she met Sean Penn, she participated in a read-through with other members of the cast — and she was sick with the flu! Kristen told *Interview* magazine that she spent most of the time gurgling and "sniffing every five seconds." It wouldn't have been so bad if she hadn't been reading huge passages of dialogue! At that time, she read the part of the narrator role, which later went to actress Jena Malone.

The real case of nerves came when Kristen went for the role of Tracy, the bohemian girl who falls for Chris. Lucky for Kristen, she didn't have sniffles that day.

"I went in and played 'Blackbird' [by the Beatles] for [Sean]," Kristen told Movie Fanatic about the experience. "That's a hard song to sing to . . . I'm not a singer. I can play it but [Sean] was really funny about it. He asked me if I didn't want him to look at me. 'Do you want me to turn around?' 'No, you have to see it.' But I'd never done anything like that."

Kristen loved doing something different for the film. She's a huge music fan. "Music is one of the most emotionally expressive things you can do," she says. In fact, her favorite kind of music is rock and roll. Cream, Led Zeppelin, Rolling Stones, Nirvana, and Green Day are some of her faves.

"I was raised on classic rock. My parents are kind of old rocker/hippie kind of people," Kristen told TeenHollywood.com. Before *Into the Wild*, Kristen's only real "music" experience was singing along with the radio and making up songs on her guitar. (She's played the instrument since she was a kid.)

So you can imagine how shocked Kristen was when it came time to film her singing scenes in *Into the Wild*. She prepared to sing one song that was already in the script (a 1971 song by John Prine called "Angel from Montgomery"). But then Kristen had the chance to write her very own song with the music director David Baerwald. It was a fantastic opportunity!

"[David and Sean] wanted a simple love song or something that a young girl would write. They said I should just go see where it takes me." Kristen was floored by the experience, unlike anything she'd ever collaborated on before.

In the movie's final credits, Kristen gets credit for all their hard work: "Tracy's Song" (the name of the tune) is listed as "Written by David Baerwald and Kristen Stewart." Drumroll, please!

Kristen felt deeply proud of her musical work on the film, although she has no plans to ditch the big screen for a recording contract any day soon.

Other than the musical experience, Kristen cherishes the many relationships she forged on the set. She got along great with leading man Emile.

"[He] Emile is one of the most confident actors I've ever worked with. [He said] 'Don't worry. Don't think about it until he calls 'action.'" When they weren't filming, they spent a lot of downtime just talking and hanging out. Of course, there wasn't a lot to do out in the middle of nowhere where they filmed.

Working with director Sean Penn was an influential experience. As Kristen told Hollywood.com, "I completely idolize [Sean] as a filmmaker. As a person, he's just great and has the most massive amount of integrity. He's great, self assured, and sure of his convictions and clear thinking."

And Sean doesn't beat around the bush. When he cast her, Sean told Kristen flat out: "I specifically wanted you." That made Kristen feel better about her part — and her acting abilities overall. Many actors agree that no matter how many performances you do, there are those moments of doubt. Everyone has them! Kristen included.

"[Sean] always says that he doesn't pull performances out of actors but he puts you somewhere where you are comfortable enough with yourself to be able to give that much. . . . He's the most gentle guy. It's easy to give him what he wants. You have a driving force. He cares so much."

Many critics (and fans) have seen Kristen's rising Hollywood star for years now. But with *Into the Wild*, they began to see the young actress really bloom. She can easily hold her own with the best actors, directors, and now songwriters. She has grown into her body, her voice, and her spirit.

"I sort of follow from [my heart]. That's what leads me," Kristen explained to Moviesonline.ca. "I don't feel like I need to get away from something. I've always been given as much freedom as I need. . . . I have that spirit in me."

With *Into the Wild*, Kristen was rewarded for her acting. She and the other members of the cast received an ensemble acting award for the movie.

After filming wrapped, Kristen did not rush into another big studio project. Instead, she acted in a few independent movies with powerful messages — and strong, self-aware girl parts. She also had a one-minute cameo as Sophie in the Hollywood blockbuster *Jumper*.

First Kristen took the role of Georgia in *The Cake Eaters*, an independent drama written by actor Jayce Bartok and directed by Mary Stuart Masterson. For Kristen, this was a chance to hook up with — and learn from — another positive role model. Mary Stuart had a hugely successful teen acting career of her own back in the 1980s. Her most famous role was Watts in *Some Kind of Wonderful*, where she played the rocker tomboy who was secretly in love with her best friend. *The Cake Eaters* is Mary Stuart's directorial debut.

Kristen and Mary Stuart really hit it off. Although *The Cake Eaters* is not an easy film, Kristen filled her role with heart and substance. She plays Georgia Kaminski, a terminally ill teenage girl wanting to experience love before it's too late. Georgia suffers from a disease call Friedreich's ataxia, which causes total deterioration of muscle control. "[My character is] fighting for that last bit of independence from her mother and she wants to do one thing on her own before she dies . . . so she picks a guy," Kristen told Movieline.com. "It's a really nice, optimistic, triumphant [life] story and I love it. Mary Stuart really did a phenomenal job. I love her, too. She's amazing."

The admiration was not one-sided. During an interview at the Newport Film Festival, Mary Stuart said of Kristen, "I really would love to see [Kristen] get an award nomination for this part . . . she is amazing in it! People always ask where we found this disabled girl to play the part. . . . Everyone is amazed that she is not really disabled."

After the role of Georgia, Kristen played Martine in a drama called *The Yellow Handkerchief.* The movie costarred William Hurt and Maria Bello and premiered at the Sundance Film Festival. It's a story of a man named Brett (played by Hurt) who has just been released from prison. He hooks up with two wandering teens — and tries to make his way back to the woman he loves. Martine and Gordy (played by British actor Eddie Redmayne) are the teens who give him a ride to New Orleans, Louisiana.

"Lately I've tried a bunch of different stuff," Kristen told MTV, "but this is what I'm really into. [*The Yellow Handkerchief* is] character driven, really quirky, sensitive, and sweet."

After filming on this wrapped, Kristen was cast as Zoe, Robert DeNiro's misfit daughter in the feature film *What Just Happened?* It's the story of the back-stabbing side of Hollywood. Kristen's role in the film is small (she clocks in around seven minutes of screen time). But she couldn't turn down the chance to star opposite the legendary DeNiro!

Starring with DeNiro in *What Just Happened?* is Sean Penn, which could explain her casting in the picture. After all, Sean was Kristen's biggest fan after her work on his movie *Into the Wild*. In life, sometimes *who* you know helps to get you from one role to the next. There are definitely six (or fewer!) degrees of separation in Hollywood.

When director Catherine Hardwicke saw Kristen's *Into the Wild* performance, along with some of her more recent independent film work, she observed that Kristen had really "blossomed." She knew that Kristen was the right actress for her new movie. And so, in early 2007, thanks to the string of performances that had preceded her, Kristen was cast in the breakout role of a lifetime. She was chosen to play leading lady Bella in the movie *Twilight*.

Kristen had assumed leading roles before *Twilight*.

But this time, she landed the main part in a film that had a huge budget — and a built-in audience. This could only mean one thing: Kristen Stewart's rising star was beginning to shine brighter than ever.

And for someone who craved anonymity, everything was about to change.

Chapter 10

Twilight Time: A Breakout Book and a Breakout Role (At Last)

In the world of publishing, everyone's looking for the next Harry Potter. Amazingly, author Stephenie Meyer seems to have written the next big thing. She created her own blockbuster book series with the young adult novel *Twilight* and its sequels: *New Moon*, *Eclipse*, and *Breaking Dawn*. The books have been number one on the *New York Times* bestseller list and have more than eleven million copies in print. Over the past few years, *Twilight* has grown into a cultural phenomenon, with a fanatic base of fans who eagerly await the movie version.

Kristen Stewart is embarrassed to admit that when she first received the script for *Twilight*, sent to her via director Catherine Hardwicke, she did not know about the book. She had not read it or even heard of it. "I must have been living under the biggest boulder ever," she joked. Of course, once she read the material, she was hooked. Kristen wanted to play the part of Bella Swan.

Twilight is a love story between two teens, one of whom happens to be a vampire.

Bella has just moved to the rainy town of Forks, Montana, to live with her dad. (Her mom is on the road with her stepdad, a minor league baseball player.) Once there, she encounters a boy named Edward in her biology class. He is nothing like anyone she's ever met. He's super smart but he's also super sensitive. She feels like he can read her mind — and soul. He also just happens to run faster than a cougar and he can stop a moving truck with his hands. And oh yeah, he's immortal. Whoa! Bella figures it out: Edward is a genuine vampire.

The idea for the *Twilight* story came to Stephenie Meyer in a dream. She woke up in the middle of the night and could not fall back asleep. The characters of Bella and Edward were talking inside her head. That's something that happens to writers sometimes — they can't turn off the ideas until the ideas get written down. So Stephenie wrote. And wrote. Eventually she turned it all into a novel — in between the hours being a Mom.

She eventually sent off the manuscript to an agent, who plucked it from the "slush pile" (that's where manuscripts go when they don't have a personal destination, like an editor's name). Now her book could get published — for real! Publishers competed to acquire this story of twenty-first-century vampires. They believed in its originality and its heart.

What's perhaps most cool about Stephenie Meyer's vampires in *Twilight* are their "lifestyle" choices. Edward has no fangs. He doesn't drink human blood. He and his family live in Forks, hang out, and go to school. When Edward meets Bella, he decides that she is his soul mate. She is the girl he's been waiting to meet for *ninety* years.

If only there weren't so many problems with their relationship!

One: The closer the pair gets, the more Edward must resist Bella. Her smell makes him crazy — so crazy that he could kill her with the swipe of one arm.

Two: Edward's not the only guy in town. Bella's affections are being sought after by another boy named Jacob . . . who just happens to be a werewolf. Talk about complicated! Everyone knows that vampires and werewolves are enemies! This could get ugly fast.

Three: There is a group of evil vampires on the loose, too, so trouble in Forks is never really far behind. One of them, James, decides that he's going to hunt Bella for sport. So Edward has to protect her.

Meyer's original film deal for *Twilight* had a script that was way more like a rock video than a novel adaptation. But then Catherine Hardwicke came on board, and the *Twilight* screenplay was rewritten (almost exactly) like the books. That's a very good thing for the fans who can be extra picky — and angry when it comes to book characters they know and love.

These days, when a book series is a success, fans often log onto YouTube and upload short videos that talk about their "dream cast" when the movie is made (*if* it is made). Before *Twilight* was officially cast, fans were already throwing out names of actresses they wanted (and pictured) in the role of Bella. When the announcement came that Kristen would be taking the part, not all fans were too happy. (Note: Stephenie Meyer's biggest fans call themselves "Twi-hards," a play on the word die-hards.)

Author Stephenie Meyer wanted to make all her "Twi-hards," or "Twilighters" (another popular expression with fans) happy. She posted this on her website shortly after Kristen got the part:

"For every actress that has been suggested as Bella in the past few years, there are always a slew of critics that cry, 'But she doesn't look like Bella!' (Which can often be translated thusly: 'She doesn't look like ME!') To this I would like to say: 'Of course she doesn't!' Bella is a fictional character, and she looks different to everyone. As is the same with every actor who will be cast in the next few months, no one is going to match up with your mental picture exactly — or mine. The thing to hope for is a really great actor who can make us believe she is Bella (or Alice or so forth) for roughly two hours. I think we've got that with Kristen Stewart, and I can't wait to see her step into the role!

"[Kristen] is an amazing actress with experience all across the board — action, horror, comedy, romance, and more. Since *Twilight* has moments that fit into every one of these genres, I'm thrilled to have a Bella who has practice with them all."

Those words came as a great relief to Kristen, who was deciding how to handle the role of Bella. She wanted to get it exactly right — for Stephenie, for director Catherine Hardwicke, for her costars, and most of all for the legions of fans! After filming ended in May 2008, Kristen said, "I feel like it was a big responsibility and I was really intimidated for a while, but now that it's done . . . I feel good. I'm really proud. I've never worked so hard on another movie."

As casting choices for *Twilight* continued to be revealed, they continued to be met with similar choruses of "What if?" or "Oh, no, not her!" commentary. Everyone seemed to have a better idea about who should play the movie roles — even for Robert Pattinson! His casting as Edward received a lot of *mixed* feedback right from the start, just like Kristen. But the young actors playing Bella and Edward soon

BSS   Behind-the-Scenes Secret

Kristen Stewart and *Twilight* author Stephenie Meyer have more in common than just the character of Bella Swan. They are both HUGE music lovers. In fact, Stephenie comes up with a playlist for each book that she writes, with bands ranging from Linkin Park to the U.K. band Muse. She also loves the band Blue October, who headlined when she traveled around for a *Breaking Dawn* joint book/rock concert tour.

won over fans. Just check out their photograph on an *Entertainment Weekly* magazine cover and you can see the intense stare and pale skin that make Robert otherworldly and totally crushable. And Kristen, too! She's simply swooning. You can almost sense the energy between them.

After a few months of announcements about individual roles, the production team finally announced the movie cast in its entirety. The roster of actors reads like a who's who of young, up-and-coming talent:

- **Kristen Stewart (Bella Swan): high school junior, new to Forks, in love with Edward**
- **Robert Pattinson (Edward Cullen): 108-year-old vampire who looks 17 and can read minds — especially Bella's**
- **Peter Facinelli (Carlisle Cullen): 400-year-old vampire who looks like he's in his mid-20s. He's the doctor in Forks, and dad to all the other Cullen family members.**

- **Elizabeth Reaser (Esme Cullen):** Carlisle's vampire wife and mom to all the Cullens
- **Ashley Greene (Alice Cullen):** Edward's sister, married to Jasper; can see the future
- **Jackson Rathbone (Jasper Hale):** has the ability to control other people's emotions, but sometimes he has trouble controlling his own hunger — for blood
- **Nikki Reed (Rosalie Cullen):** the most beautiful person alive, married to Emmett
- **Kellan Lutz (Emmett Cullen):** muscle-head vampire who adores Rosalie

Once filming on *Twilight* began, fans seemed pleased with the casting choices and how things were working out. No one, however, was more pleased than Kristen. She immersed herself in the part of Bella. With this portrayal she wanted to "do right by" the fans who love the books.

"Bella is a very honest . . . straight-up, good-natured girl who found herself in an insane position . . . [She's] seemingly logical, and then all of the sudden she's thinking of herself as a psychotic person and [she's] just swept away by something more powerful than her. Every girl wants to lose herself. . . . I could relate to her," Kristen told *Premiere* magazine at Comic Con (the conference to present new movies, books, games, and more into the market).

On YouTube, blogs, and message boards, fans continued to seek out any new information they could find about the making of the movie or about its stars. They were hungry for all the vampire/love story information they could sink their teeth into.

Kristen began to realize that she'd accepted a role that was not only interesting on its own, within the context of the *Twilight* storyline, but this was a role that could change the entire tone of her career. The role could be "the one!"

All her other movie experiences had led Kristen to this most enviable position. She was poised on the edge of superstardom, but it had not happened overnight. She'd worked hard, tried many different kinds of roles, and challenged herself in the company of popular and legendary actors and actresses. Although she was still only seventeen (she actually turned eighteen while filming *Twilight*!) this was an actress who was, as many had said before, wise and talented beyond her years. She could even fly. Well, sort of. Edward — and that special effects team — had a little something to do with it.

Kristen explained an especially crazy *Twilight* scene to MTV: "[Robert] throws me over his back [in one scene], right before he's going to tell me that he's a vampire, and then he runs over the treetops. And [we were] in real treetops . . . not just CGI. . . . We actually [got] to go up there, and that's what I'm stoked on."

In another interview with *TV Guide*, Kristen explained, "Bella starts off as a pretty logical, sort of objective girl and gets swept away by something she never thought imaginable."

Swept away, for sure.

Just like the fans — who began spreading crazy rumors about Kristen and Robert.

Fan sites claimed that Robert and Kristen were a real-life couple — because they seemed so close in their on-screen relationship. They also knew how to have a good time in interviews. And Robert didn't help matters much when he told *Seventeen* magazine that his celeb crush was Kristen Stewart — and that he dreams about her, too!

But the truth is that all the rumors are just that, *rumors*. There was no offscreen love story here. This was a case of two excellent young actors making a very real connection — and giving it back to audiences.

And what it meant was that *Twilight* was going to be an awesome movie experience.

Chapter 11

Kristen and Robert: A Dream Couple

Director Catherine Hardwicke had been impressed with the chemistry between Kristen and Robert from the first audition. She told *Entertainment Weekly* about the first time the two staged a scene together. It was a love scene, of course, and "It was electric! The room shorted out, the sky opened up, and I was like, 'This is going to be good.'"

Both actors came into the movie with an intensity that really pops off the screen. They wanted their performances to be unguarded. Each day of the 45-day movie shoot was loaded with not only chemistry — but deep emotion.

On set, Kristen often took extra time before shooting an emotional scene. As an actress, she likes to be alone in between takes so she can dig deep and find the source of a character's joy or sadness. She knows how to produce emotion for the screen. As Bella, sometimes Kristen gets so emotional that she cries for each take, but she makes sure there is nothing fake in her work. She wants every scene to be an amazing transformation, as if Kristen has literally *become* Bella.

Robert (aka Rob on set) is the designated good guy, the one who usually comes over to help shake Kristen out of any intense moment. On set, he's a little bit like Kristen's lifeline, patting her back or whispering in her ear. They have developed a very special chemistry working together. These two acting professionals have found a rhythm and respect for each other that works.

How did they keep their connection so strong? From the moment the actors first got the *Twilight* script, they met together to see how it felt reading through the material. During all of preproduction, they spent an intense amount of time together, reading lines, sharing stories, and exchanging personal information. They worked hard to get to the core of the "Romeo and Juliet" romance vibe in the story.

It seems like they got it right.

One of the most romantic scenes in the movie between Edward and Bella is the moment when Bella goes to the Cullen home for the first time. He plays a lullaby for Bella on his grand piano. Fortunately for fans — and for Robert — director Hardwicke allowed Edward to write his very own song! The *Twilight* ballad is called "Bella's Song." And it's really no surprise that Robert did a good job writing it. That's because he has a small band of his own in London, England, called "Bad Girl." (Now *that* band name sounds a little dangerous and very *Edward*, doesn't it?)

In addition to knowing music, Robert knows about being a heartthrob.

As Cedric Diggory in *Harry Potter and the Goblet of Fire*, he played a Hufflepuff prefect who was actually close to *perfect*. Cedric competed with Harry for the Triwizard Tournament title and for the affections of Cho Chang at the Yule Ball. But, alas, Cedric got into some trouble. And — spoiler alert if you haven't seen it or read it yet — Cedric dies. Talk about intense. It was hard *not* to love Robert in that role! In fact, when that Harry Potter flick premiered in England, twelve *thousand* screaming girls turned out in Leicester Square for Robert's autograph.

When he headed to Oregon to film *Twilight*, Robert decided to ignore all the fuss fans had raised about whether or not he'd make a good Edward. Instead, he wanted to get serious and focused. He even brought a personal trainer with him to the set and planned to run each morning at five A.M.! For him, the acting process is still a huge learning curve. He explained to *Wonderland* magazine, "The acting's come along by accident. I've never trained or anything, so I've only very recently become even vaguely comfortable with it. On *Harry Potter* I was so conscious of the fact that I didn't know what I was doing, I used to sit on the side of the set throwing up." Robert says he's considering going back to study acting in school, but the truth is, he already has all the right instincts.

Robert admits that originally what he liked best about assuming the part of Edward was the *lack* of information available to him about the 108-year-old vampire. He figured he could create whatever persona he wanted, not knowing the backstory that author Meyer had in mind. But as he prepared for the role, he needed more. *Twilight* is told from Bella's perspective, so Kristen had more original material in the screenplay and books to help her understand her character better.

What about Robert? He got something special from author Meyer.

After writing the fourth book in her *Twilight* saga, Meyer had penned a sort of *Twilight* sequel called *Midnight Sun* with the same plot as *Twilight*, but told from Edward's point of view instead of Bella's point of view. Edward explained to MTV, "It's exactly the same events, but a couple of other things happen. . . . It's funny how different things affect Edward in ways that you really don't expect if you have just read *Twilight.*"

Midnight Sun was a cool concept, and it certainly helped Rob to get a good grasp of the character of Edward. It would certainly be a big book for fans, too! But at the end of summer 2008, something devastating happened to Stephenie Meyer. The *Midnight Sun* document was *leaked* online! Meyer was furious — and extremely hurt. She wrote on her site in late August, "I feel too sad about what has happened to continue working on *Midnight Sun*, and so it is on hold indefinitely. I'd rather my fans not read this version. It was only an incomplete draft; the writing is messy and flawed and full of mistakes."

Meyer said one day she may publish it online for herself and the fans. But publish or not, she hoped it had served its most important purpose. The hefty manuscript helped Rob to get that much closer to the thoughts and actions of Edward. It helped to make the *Twilight* movie that much more intense for viewers — and for Kristen.

Meyer agreed that her vision of the two young characters had been realized in *Twilight*. After viewing a rough cut of the film for the first time, the author told *Rolling Stone* magazine, "[The movie] just has the soul of the book . . . Bella and Edward's relationship."

You can't beat something with soul.

Chapter 12

The Fan-nomenon Continues: After *Twilight*

For the fans, breaking down what makes Kristen's new flick a sure thing is as e-z as one, two, three. So far in her career, Kristen has gotten universal praise for her acting. What she's needed was a breakthrough, commercial success. *Twilight* the movie seems to have it all:

1. **An incredible cast (Led by Kristen, of course!)**
2. **Loads of vampires (Dangerous *and* friendly)**
3. **Crazy love (Sigh! Gasp! Wow!)**

Director Hardwicke says she always knew *Twilight* would be a compelling — if not challenging — movie. But she also knew it would be a great opportunity for her young stars. As she told MTV, "I got swept away into the feeling of this whole, almost obsessive love. A

Twilight the movie isn't just about the romance. There are some kick-butt action sequences, too. Hardwicke hired storyboard artists who had worked on *The Matrix* to help visualize action scenes like the moment in Port Angeles when Edward rescues Bella. The film has its own action director, too, Andy Cheng. Cheng has flipped and chopped and kicked his way through numerous movies over the years, mostly as superstar Jackie Chan's stunt double. Cheng's favorite thing to do? Wirework! That's where the actor is attached to a wire so it appears like the character is almost flying. Cheng especially loves choreographing fight scenes in midair!

really cool teenager, just falling madly in love, so in love with this guy that she would actually turn into a vampire to be with him. And I thought: 'That's kinda great.' And [then] I thought, 'How visual!' These vampires live in the forest. We've never seen anything like that. We've never seen vampires playing baseball — superhuman-vampire-speed baseball. There were so many challenges, you know?"

As the days and weeks until the movie's opening draw closer, the fan-nomenon that is *Twilight* just continues to grow. When the most recent book, *Breaking*

Dawn, was released, Hachette Book Group announced that they had sold 1.3 million copies at midnight the very first day it went on sale! The audience just keeps getting bigger — and expectation for the film keeps getting bigger, too.

When, at the end of summer, it was announced that the movie's release had been moved *up*, fan expectation grew even higher — and hotter. Originally scheduled for a December 12 release date, the film was moved up nearly a month to a November release. Now *Twilight* the movie would get one of the best blockbuster opening weekends available. Opening around the Thanksgiving holiday would mean gobbling up all of the competition for sure!

How could Kristen possibly prepare for the movie's release — and all the hype that goes with it? She says, "You can't overthink that kind of stuff or you just end up messing yourself up." So she stayed mostly mum about anticipation for the film, doing the required interviews and focusing instead on her character. After all, there's the possibility of at least three more movies starring Bella and the others.

No one else stayed too mum, though. Magazines and the blogosphere have been leaking *Twilight* details and stories for months. Throughout the production process, MTV's website devoted an entire blog to the production and release of the *Twilight* movie. Every Tuesday was called "*Twilight* Tuesday" on the site, and featured video clips and interviews with the cast.

One of the most impressive things about the *Twilight* phenomenon is how vast its fan base has become. There are numerous links on the *Twilight* home page, too, about where fans can go to get up-to-the-minute facts about the flick, including:

http://www.stepheniemeyer.com/
http://www.thetwilightsaga.com/

And the movie isn't just for English-speaking audiences. Kristen's brave performance as Bella will be seen all over the world. She'll soon be a major international star! So far there are already *Twilight* movie and fan sites in countries including Argentina, Australia, Brazil, Chile, Colombia, Finland, France, Italy, Mexico, the Philippines, Portugal, Spain, Switzerland, and Venezuela. Coming soon: even more countries in Asia and Europe!

According to the Twilight Topsites, there are now

more than eighty-six websites dedicated to Stephenie Meyer's book and movie, *Twilight*. Whoa! That list is, of course, still growing. And it's not just high school girls who are the fans. There are college students, working moms, stay-at-home moms, grandmothers, and plenty of male "Twi-hards," too. There will probably be even more guy fans once the movie — with all of its CGI and cool action sequences — gets played in theaters.

Just think: All those people will now know the star power of Kristen Jaymes Stewart. From the dreidel song back in elementary school to "Bella's Song" on the big screen, Kristen has continued to blaze a path.

And with *Twilight*, it seems confirmed: Kristen is indeed the belle of the ball.

Chapter 13

Future Shock: Kristen's Next Moves

When asked what she wanted to do next, now that *Twilight* was done, Kristen quipped, "I never know what I'm doing next until I'm standing on my mark with a mic on."

However, Kristen also told MTV that she thought *Twilight* was "a pretty triumphant love story . . . and it deserves to be a series of three."

Can you say *sequel*? You can almost hear the fans cheering already.

Unfortunately there have been no official announcements about *Twilight* sequels from director Hardwicke or Summit Entertainment — *yet*.

Producer Greg Mooradian told the press and MTV, "[A sequel has] been discussed . . . I can't tell you we're at that place yet, but it's definitely been discussed. . . .

We would like to give the audience a sense of knowing that the next installment is going to come at a really specific increment of time."

So what's *really* coming up next?

More acting, and with a few non-vampires this time.

Recently, Kristen wrapped up production on a new flick coming out next summer 2009. It's called *Adventureland*. She stars in the movie with Ryan Reynolds and independent actor Jesse Eisenberg. It's directed by Greg Mottola, who helmed the super-hit *Superbad*, with Michael Cera and Jonah Hill. They shot the film in Pittsburgh, Pennsylvania, but it's based on the director's real-life experiences working at a Long Island, New York, park.

Adventureland is set during the summer of 1987. It's the story of a tightly wound, stuffy college graduate (played by Eisenberg) who realizes he can't afford his dream vacation to Europe. What does he do? He takes a minimum-wage job at the local amusement park. The experience forces him to loosen up and surprisingly he finds new friendships and . . . LOVE! Kristen plays Em, his romantic interest.

Seems like Kristen is really on a roll with romantic parts now!

Kristen told IGN that what she loves best about making *Adventureland* was that she knows "these kids and their stories. [Mottola's] characters don't seem comedic, but rather are such real human beings. It's not like watching a sensationalized version of your teenage life."

Currently, Kristen is also filming a movie now called *Welcome to the Rileys*, with Emmy Award–winning actor James Gandolfini. (Most folks know him as Tony Soprano from the hit HBO show *The Sopranos*.) In the flick, Kristen plays the serious part of Mallory who, hold on to your hat, plays a girl who works in a bar and has a relationship with an older man! Whoa! Actually, as the movie progresses, her character discovers that the man is more of a father figure to her and she becomes a part of his family. It's a complicated story about what makes a family — and how to find love. And it's definitely a part that will bring Kristen a different measure of critical attention for her performance skill — and range.

Of course, acting is not all Kristen has in the cards for her future.

More than anything else — even more than acting — Kristen says she wants to *write* — and maybe head back to school, too.

"My family is all movie people and I really love what I'm doing right now. But I definitely want to go to school. I want to be a writer. That's what I'm really into. My mom is Australian, so I might go to university in Sydney. I can't wait.

"I'm not like Jodie Foster or Mary Stuart Masterson, or some of the other women I've worked with, who are almost compulsive doers. They're just powerhouses. I like focusing on one thing and taking it slow. When I'm at school I think I might just be at school."

When recently interviewed by Movies Online, Kristen also talked at length about writing versus acting. She acknowledged that both offer a huge rush — of emotion, excitement, accomplishment. But they have a hugely different effect on her.

"There's something really instantaneous the second you do a scene and you feel it and it's so real for you and you know it's down and you nailed it. It's so amazing just because you've told the story and you did it. It just feels so good. But writing is more self-indulgent."

By self-indulgent, Kristen means that it takes a little more digging and deep thought to make it happen. Writing is a process of going inside and making up a world or a life that truly matters to other people. She likes that process a lot.

If she woke up tomorrow and could no longer act, there's no doubt in Kristen's mind that she'd continue to do something in showbiz — no matter what. "If I had to have a practical job, if acting fell through, I couldn't imagine working anywhere but on a movie set. I would want to work in props or the art department."

But her first choice would be to write screenplays. Perhaps it's in the genes? After all, her mom, Jules, is already a successful writer, script doctor, and so much more.

One time, Kristen told *Girl's Life* magazine that if she had a choice between truth or dare, she'd pick truth every time. That's the sign of a born storyteller. She isn't afraid to dig around for details.

"I am just a lover of words, putting them together . . . I think I'd rather write short stories and maybe, who knows, I would love to write a novel . . . I write with a friend, too, which is awesome. It's like the first time that

I've ever been able to. I don't really want to get into it, but it's awesome. I sort of have a writing partner and I also do it by myself. I kind of always have."

Acting? Writing? What does Kristen's family think about their daughter's numerous career options?

Kristen told *Interview* magazine, "[My parents and I] haven't really overanalyzed my acting career or even my academic career. It's totally up in the air, which I think is the best position for me to be in right now. It's just sort of like, 'We'll see.'"

Fans everywhere will be waiting to see what this rising star does next, too.

Chapter 14

More Fun Facts:
Everything You Need To Know!

Birth name: Kristen Jaymes Stewart

Nickname(s): Kris, KStew

Date of birth: April 9, 1990

Place of birth: Los Angeles, California (she lived for a
    while in Colorado, too)

Height: 5' 6" (1.68 m)

Eyes: Green (although she wore contact lenses to get
    Bella's brown-eyed stare in *Twilight*)

Hair: Light brown (natural color) although she's dyed it
    dark and blond a few times for movies

Father: John Stewart

Mother: Jules Mann Stewart

Brother: Cameron Stewart

Pets: She and her mom have 3 dogs: Oz, a border collie mix; Jack and Lily, who are mutts.

School: Laurel Springs Distance Learning School

Favorite subject: Literature (she'd love to study Shakespeare)

Advice from Mom and Dad: "They've always been really supportive . . . Basically [they tell me] 'You just have to make yourself happy and you've got to do what you want to do.' And they're just really motivating, sort of a driving force, which is something I really need."

How she chooses roles: "I'm just drawn to stories that I can personally connect with. I never planned it. I'm not saying anything like, 'Young girls, stand up and yell!' It's not that I consciously sought after these roles but I'm naturally drawn to them."

On the red carpet: "It's overwhelming. You almost want

to run away . . . I'm not into large groups of people."

Advice for fans: "People always ask actors for advice and it's like, Wow, you're asking us? I don't know how enlightening we can be. We're just people."

On growing up: "Being young is frustrating. It drives me kind of insane. I feel so restricted. I can't wait to get to the stage where I can wake up in the morning and just do what I want."

Clothing picks before *Twilight*: Levi's, Chuck Taylor Converse sneakers, anything that's beat-up. "I kind of like to look like a hobo. How about anarchist pixie?"

Clothing picks after *Twilight*: She recently appeared at an MTV event wearing all Gucci, a top designer!

Trademark fashion statement: She wears several black rubber bracelets around her left wrist. She says they're always on because the bracelets are too tough to get off!

Best pampering moment to date: On a model shoot with
photographer Bruce Weber for *Teen Vogue*, the
crew brought in a masseuse just for Kristen to
get massages during the shoot!

Modeling experience: *Teen Vogue, Cosmo Girl, Vanity Fair, Jalouse, Elle, Italian Vogue* (they did
an awesome feature with Kristen and her older
brother Cameron)

Commercial experience: She appeared in GAP ads with
the slogan "Long live individuality" (sounds like
Kristen, for sure!)

Music and dance: "I love forties Big Bands like swing
music and I started taking swing lessons and I go
to Arthur Murray dance studio!"

Future rock star? She plays the guitar, but says, "No,
I would rather just play with my friends." One
time her parents gave her a classic record player
(and LPs, or records!) because she loves classic
rock so much.

Hot stuff? In 2008, she was chosen as #18 on Movie
Fanatic's top 20 Hot & Favorite actresses list.
She was also ranked #17 on *Entertainment
Weekly's* "30 Under 30" actress list.

Directors she wants to work with? Martin Scorsese
("I'm sure everyone says that.")

Actors she admires? Heath Ledger, Paul Dano, Emile
Hirsch, Evan Rachel Wood, Natalie Portman, and
Jodie Foster (of course)

Favorite movies of all time? *ET, Spaceballs, The Shining, Immortal Beloved,* stuff by Buster Keaton.
"There are so many movies, I could just sit here
and rattle them off. . . ."

What she does in her free time: " A lot of people are
like, 'Ah, you must be so busy. What do you get
to do in your rare minutes of alone time?' I
have so much time off. I'm pretty boring. I read
a lot. I watch a lot of movies. I hang out with
my brother."

Favorite hobby: Surfing!

Other hobbies: "I read a lot of books, and I'm a writer. That's what I'm mainly into. I just love putting the words together. I'm really in love with words. I play guitar; I love going to shows. I'm kind of a homebody."

Best way to get in touch? "I'm getting a BlackBerry. I don't even have an e-mail address. I just need a phone that's not gonna break."

On her iPod? Van Morrison, the Beatles, the Rolling Stones.

How she gets around? '95 Toyota Tacoma.

RÉSUMÉ

FILM	RELEASED	CHARACTER
Welcome to the Rileys	To be announced	Mallory
Adventureland	2009	Em
Twilight	2008	Isabella "Bella" Swan
What Just Happened?	2008	Zoe
Jumper	2008	Sophie (cameo)
The Yellow Handkerchief	2008	Martine
Cake Eaters	2007	Georgia
Into the Wild	2007	Tracy Tatro
Fierce People	2007	Maya
In the Land of Women	2007	Lucy Hardwicke
The Messengers	2007	Jess Solomon
Zathura	2005	Lisa
Speak	2005	Melinda Sordino
Undertow	2004	Lila
Catch That Kid	2004	Maddy Phillips
Cold Creek Manor	2003	Kristen Tilson
Panic Room	2002	Sarah Altman
The Safety of Objects	2002	Sam Jennings